Copyright © 2025   HARRIS, CHAD
Two Penny Publishing
1209 SE 21st Avenue
Cape Coral, FL 33990

TwoPennyPublishing.com
info@TwoPennyPublishing.com

All rights reserved. No part of this publication may be reproduced, distributed, or transmitted in any form or by any means, including photocopying, recording, or other electronic or mechanical methods, without the prior written permission of the publisher, except by a reviewer who wishes to quote brief passages in connection with a review written for inclusion in a magazine, newspaper, website, or broadcast.

ISBN: 978-1-965341-19-3

eBook also available

For information about this author, to book event appearance, or media interview, please contact the author representative at: info@twopennypublishing.com

FIRST EDITION

Two Penny Publishing is a partnership publisher of a variety of genres. We help first-time and seasoned authors share their stories, passion, knowledge, and experiences that help others grow and learn. Please visit our website: TwoPennyPublishing.com if you would like us to consider your manuscript or book idea for publishing.

Two Brothers, One Song

Written by
Chad Harris

Illustrated by
C.J. Love

Lift Every Voice and Sing

This book is dedicated to the memory of
Stormiyah Denson-Jackson,
Gerald Watson,
Karon Brown,
Jakhi Snider,
Demarcos Pinckney,
Kevin Mason,
Dar'Juan McRoy,
and Devell Wade

These children's lives were snatched far too soon. Each one was a student at Stanton Elementary in Southeast Washington, DC. They were full of promise, potential, and light. Their absence is not just a loss to their school and their families, but also a wound carried by an entire community — a reminder of the urgent need for protection, justice, and, above all, change. The weight of what was lost can never be measured. These young souls deserved long lives, filled with laughter, love, and opportunity. While their voices have been silenced, their names live on, not only in mourning but in purpose. May their memory ignite a fierce resolve to build a world where no more children are buried before they have a chance to bloom.

Written by BreeAnna Haynes on behalf of the Stanton community.

James and John Johnson were brothers so true,
supporting each other in all they would do.
Through trials and triumphs, their bond never broke.
They created an anthem and our spirits awoke.

James Johnson

John Johnson

They became leaders, inspiring us still,
with words and music that give us the will.
Through marches and tributes, through struggles and pain,
they gave us a legacy that keeps breaking chains.

James and John's mother, Helen Louise Dillet,
was raised with conviction — no one could steal it.
A devoted mother, a Stanton School teacher,
she married James Johnson, headwaiter and preacher.

Their father taught his sons how to serve others.
He led with grace, supporting the brothers.
With wisdom and strength, he'd always stand tall,
guiding his sons' paths and showing respect is for all.

Young James focused on school, wanting to learn more.
He believed in education, which helped him soar.
He knew in the future he would someday give back
to those whose opportunities seemed often to lack.

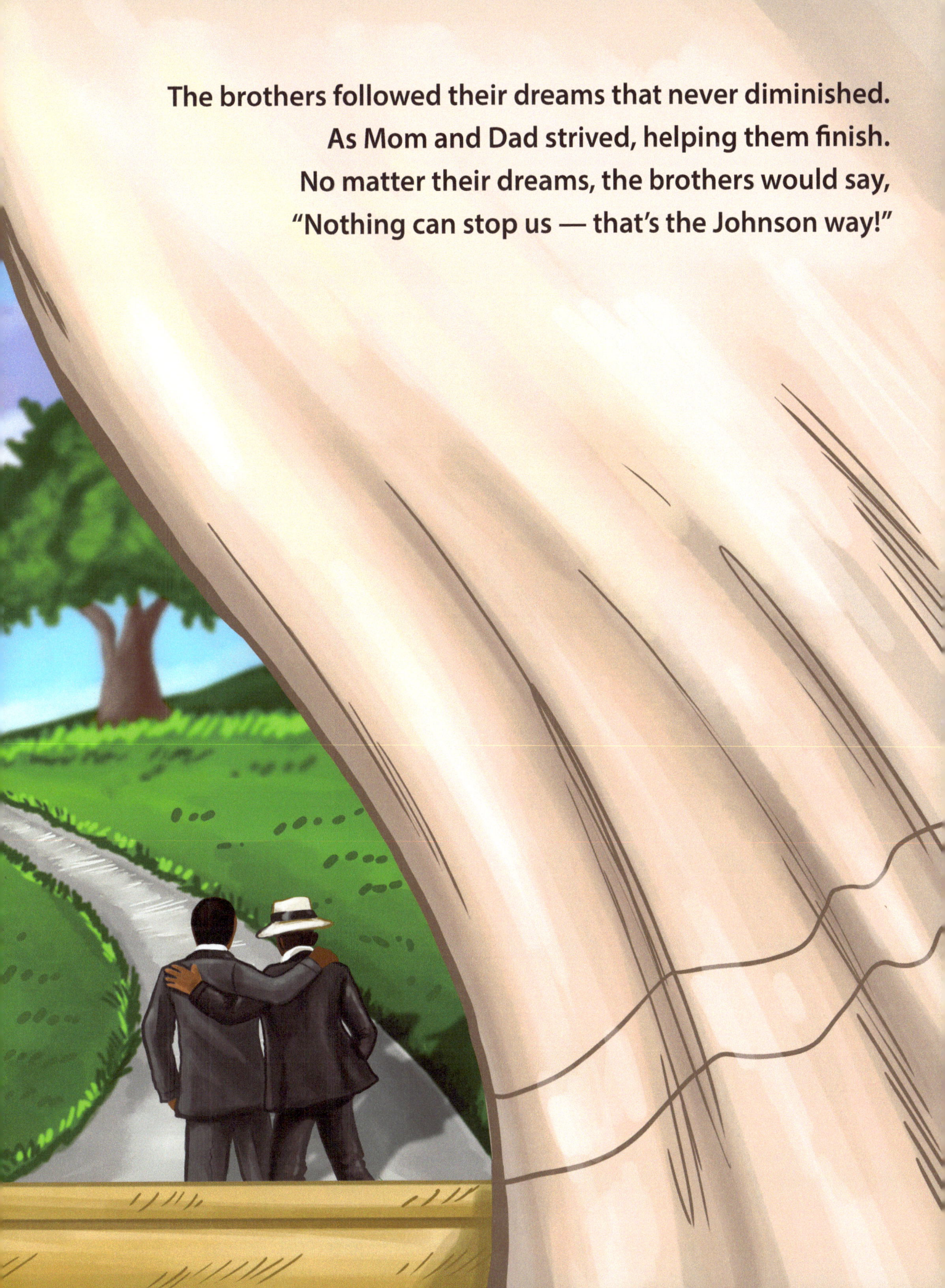

The brothers followed their dreams that never diminished.
As Mom and Dad strived, helping them finish.
No matter their dreams, the brothers would say,
"Nothing can stop us — that's the Johnson way!"

James left home with purpose and pride—
to learn, to grow, and to not be denied.
James studied writing at Atlanta University.
His words shaped culture in the face of adversity.

His freshman year, James's pathway was clear.
A summer in Georgia, his convictions grew dear.
He taught young children whose parents had been enslaved,
teaching them to read — so their futures were paved.

John, the younger brother, left for school too.
He attended a conservatory and wrote songs — quite a few.
He left for London and studied abroad,
but he needed his brother more than worldly applause.
He came back home and decided to teach.
As a music teacher, many students he'd reach.

Meanwhile, James started teaching at his mother's school.
He once was a student, now he was making the rules.
After a few years, James rose to the top,
The principal at Stanton, leading everyone nonstop.
He added more grades, so no students had to leave.
The school kept growing, leading students to achieve.

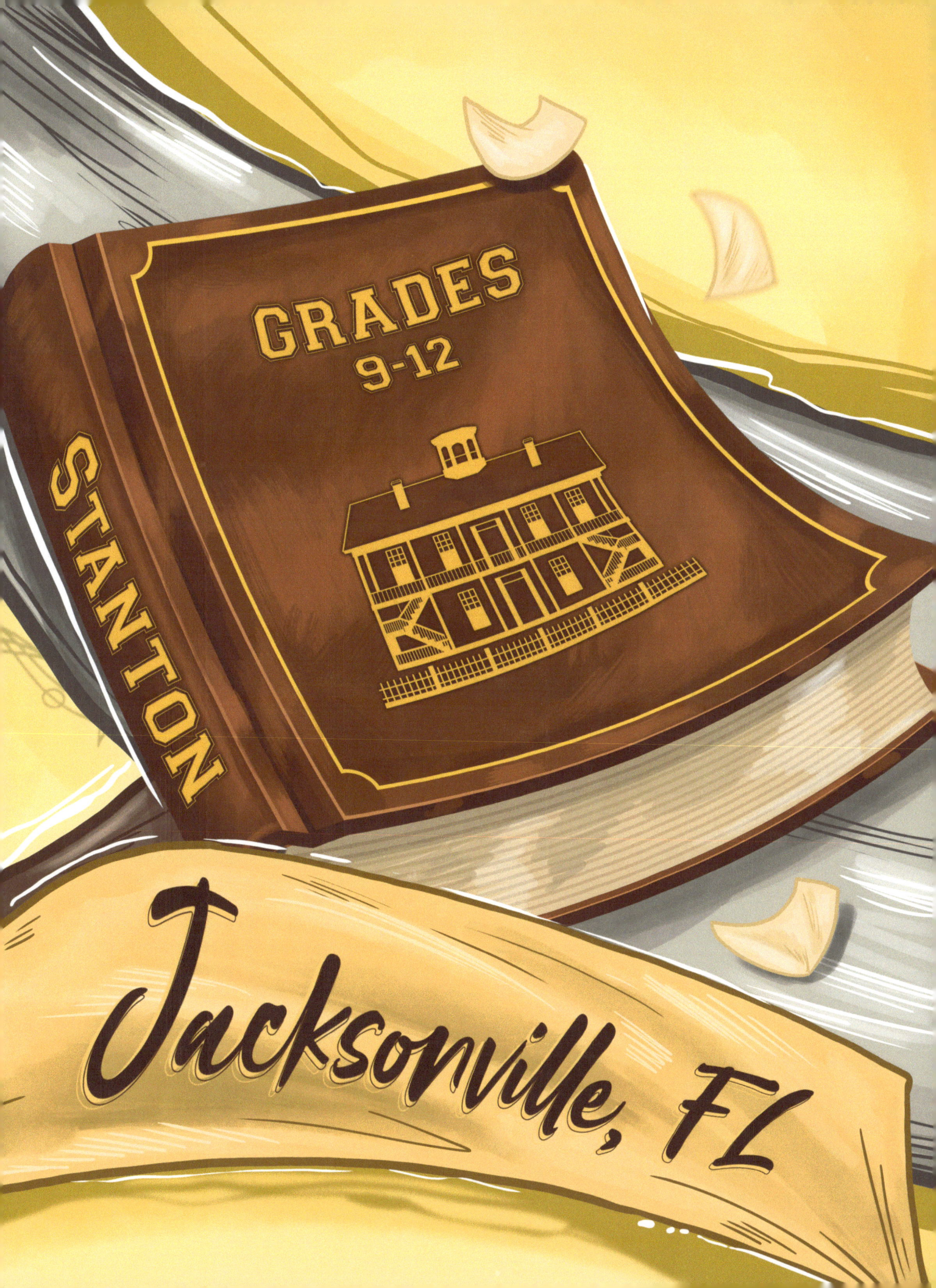

While James was teaching, his dreams grew and grew.
He started to write what his heart and mind knew.
Remembering the stories his family passed down—
a bitter past, where hatred was found.

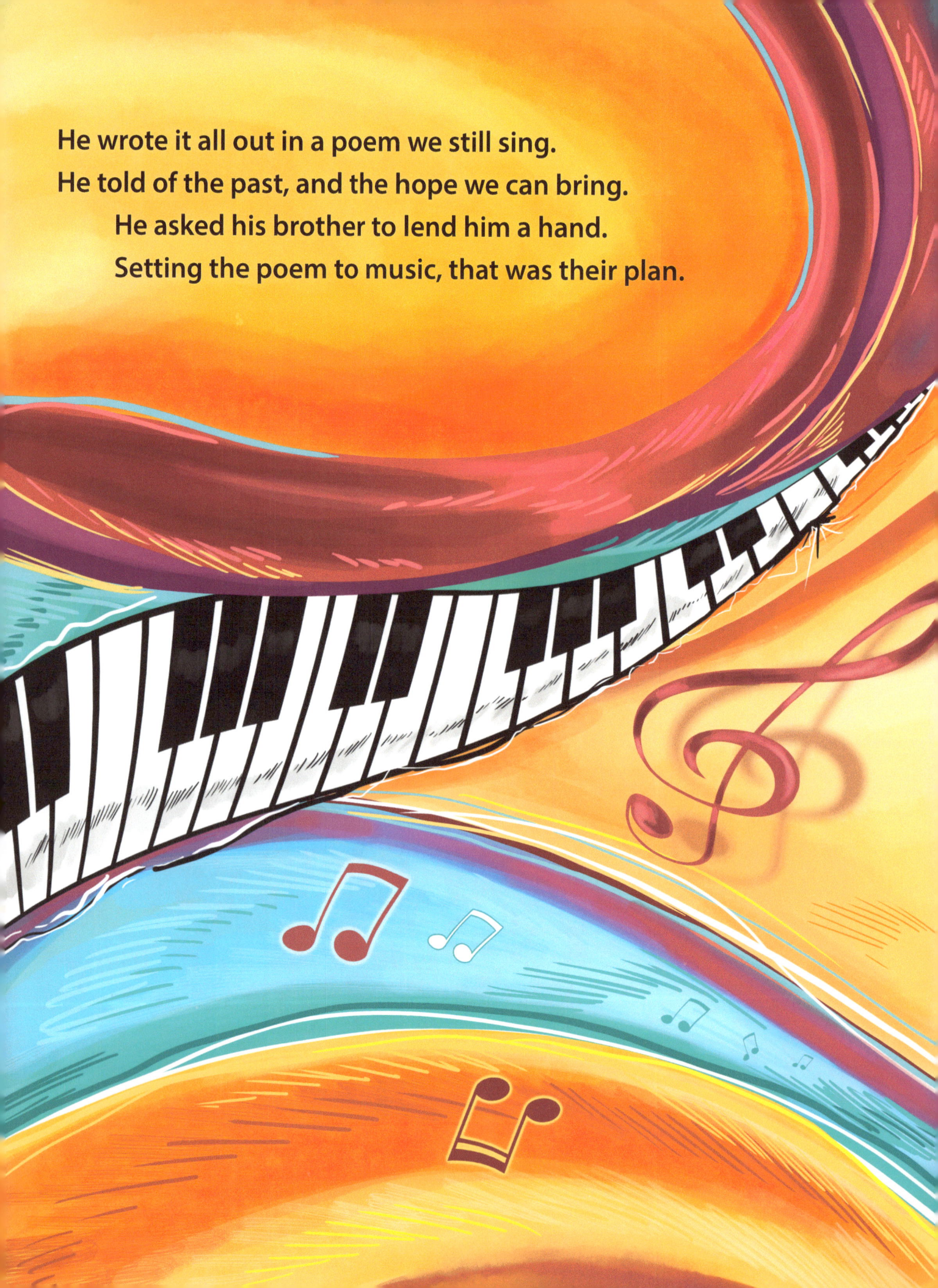

He wrote it all out in a poem we still sing.
He told of the past, and the hope we can bring.
He asked his brother to lend him a hand.
Setting the poem to music, that was their plan.

Lift every voice and sing,
'Til earth and heaven ring,
Ring with the harmonies of Liberty;
Let our rejoicing rise
High as the listening skies,
Let it resound loud as the rolling sea.
Sing a song full of the faith that the dark past has taught us,
Sing a song full of the hope that the present has brought us;
Facing the rising sun of our new day begun,
Let us march on 'til victory is won.

Inspired by their students, holding tight to their dream, the brothers worked together — they were a team. James wrote the lyrics. John added the tune. They knew this song would lift spirits soon.

Stanton students were gathered with care,
learning this song, like a deep urgent prayer.
When children sang out, they felt themselves rise.
Their voices were soaring to listening skies.
Through churches and choirs, its message took flight,
spreading hope through the day and throughout the long night.

In 1900, Booker T. Washington did speak,
to honor Lincoln's birthday, when hope still looked bleak.
As hundreds of students stood side by side,
they sang the brothers' poem with passion and pride.

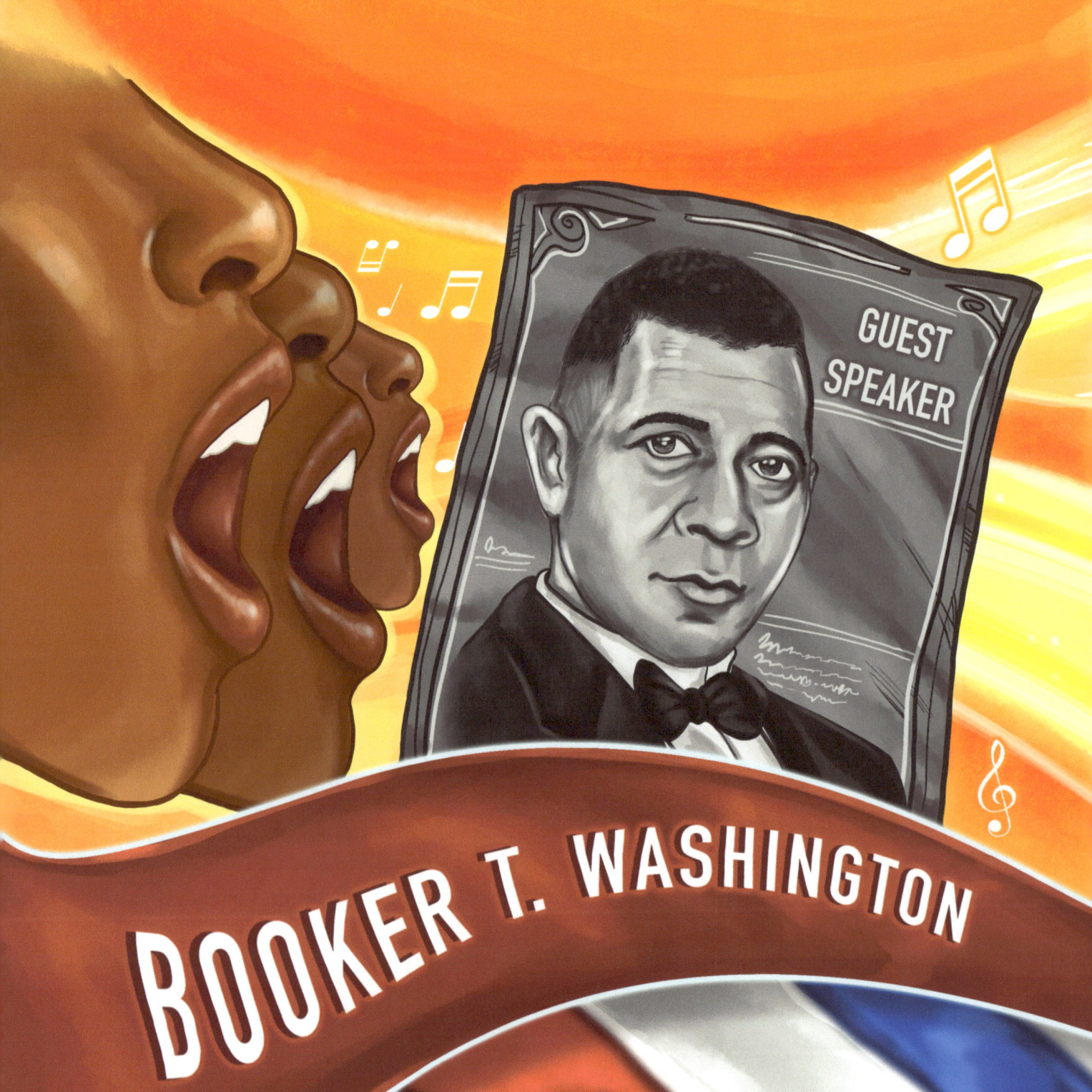

"Lift up your voice, let heaven and earth ring..."
The children started singing, filled with hope to bring.
With a steady beat, they stood on their feet.
Booker T. loved this melody that sounded so sweet.
When the students were finished, everyone was amazed
at the brothers' song, which earned them great praise.

"Lift up your voice, let heaven and earth ring..."

"Lift Every Voice and Sing," the Black anthem supreme.
These Stanton students realized the dream.
Over 125 years, we've gathered, sung, and cheered
to lift every voice, as two brothers pioneered.

James and John Johnson were brothers so true,
who created this song for me and for you.
These words, this poem, this powerful hymn—
they bring hope and a message that never will dim.

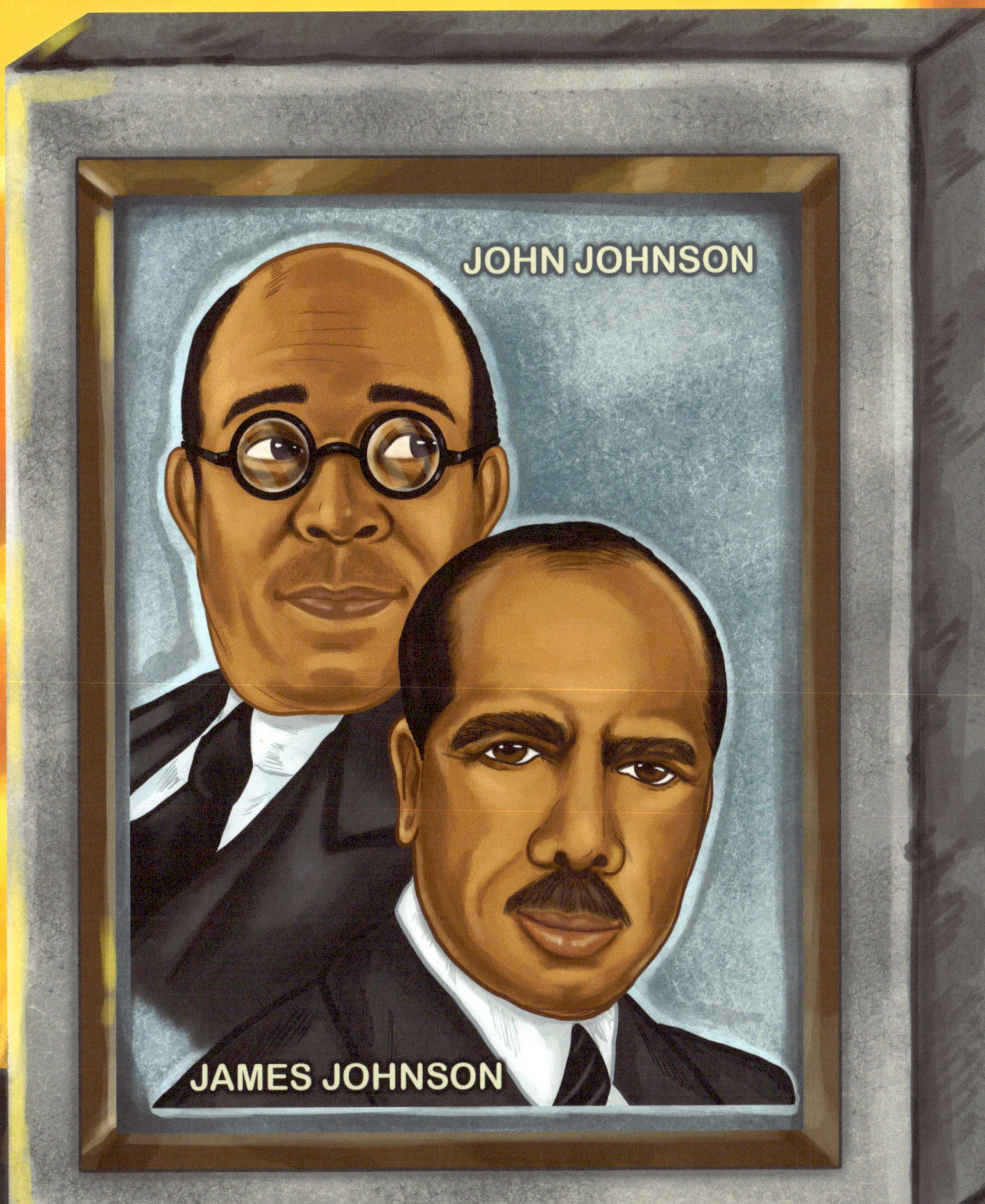

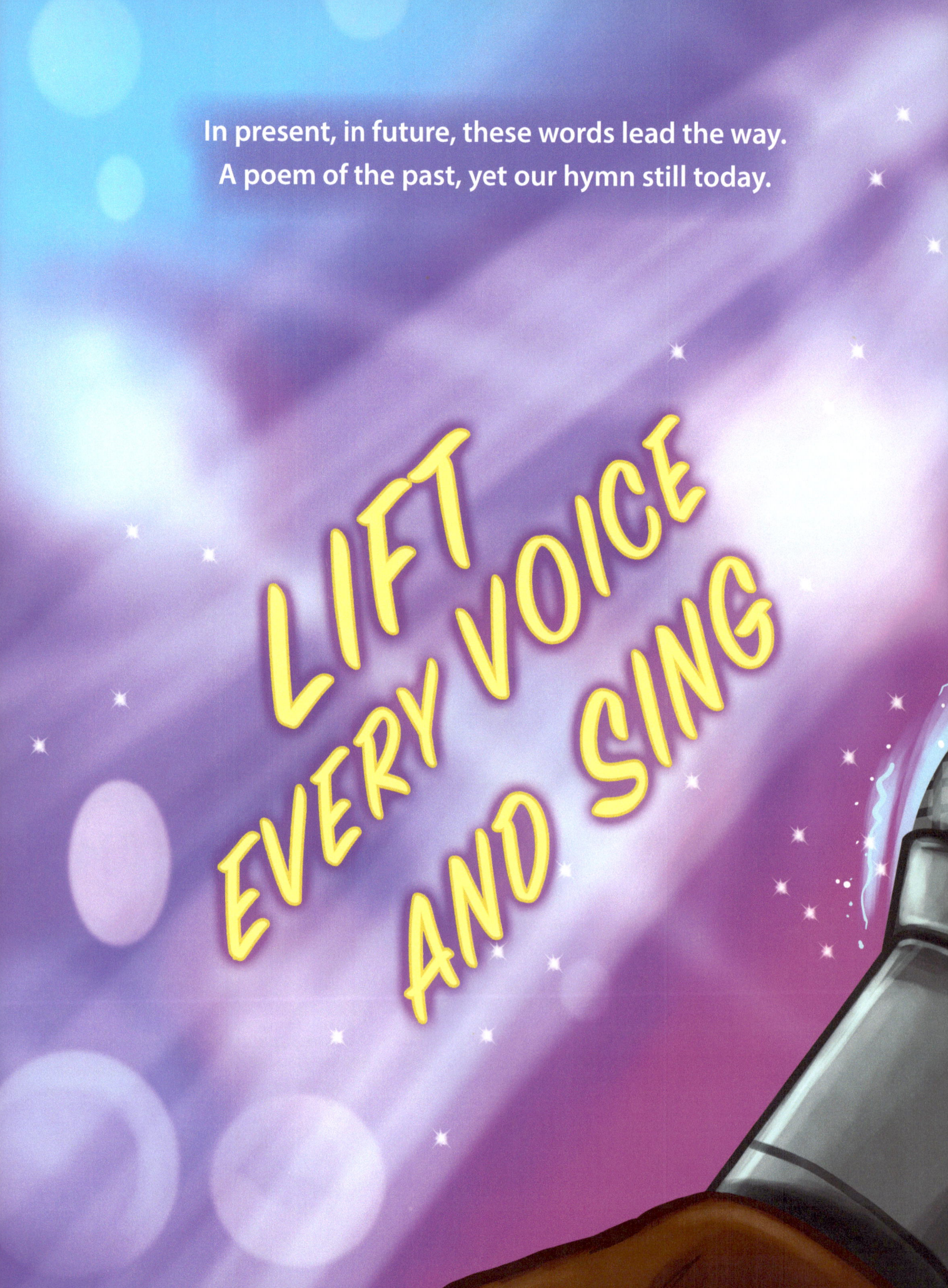

"LIFT EVERY VOICE AND SING"

Words by J. W. Johnson

Music by J. Rosamond Johnson

Lift every voice and sing,

Till earth and heaven ring,

Ring with the harmonies of Liberty;

Let our rejoicing rise

High as the list'ning skies,

Let it resound loud as the rolling sea.

Sing a song full of the faith that the dark past has taught us,

Sing a song full of the hope that the present has brought us;

Facing the rising sun of our new day begun,

Let us march on till victory is won.

Stony the road we trod,

Bitter the chast'ning rod,

Felt in the days when hope unborn had died;

Yet with a steady beat,

Have not our weary feet

Come to the place for which our fathers sighed?

We have come over a way that with tears has been watered.

We have come, treading our path through

the blood of the slaughtered,

Out from the gloomy past,

Till now we stand at last

Where the white gleam of our bright star is cast.

God of our weary years,

God of our silent tears,

Thou who hast brought us thus far on the way;

Thou who hast by Thy might,

Led us into the light,

Keep us forever in the path, we pray.

Lest our feet stray from the places, our God, where we met Thee,

Lest our hearts, drunk with the wine of the world, we forget Thee;

Shadowed beneath Thy hand,

May we forever stand,

True to our God,

True to our native land.

TIMELINE

1871 — James Weldon Johnson is born in Jacksonville, Florida.

1873 — John Rosamond Johnson is born in Jacksonville, Florida.

1887 — James graduates from Stanton School, in Jacksonville, Florida.

1890s — The brothers go to college. James studies at Atlanta University. John studies music at the New England Conservatory.

1893 — John leaves the New England Conservatory and moves to London to study music.

1894 — James graduates from Atlanta University and begins teaching at Stanton School in Jacksonville, Florida.

1895 — James starts The Daily American newspaper, the first Black-oriented newspaper in Jacksonville, Florida.

1896 — John begins teaching music in Jacksonville Public Schools, where he eventually became the music supervisor.

1897 — James becomes the first African American admitted to the Florida bar exam, which he passed while serving as a school principal.

1899 - 1900 — James and John write the lyrics and music for "Lift Every Voice and Sing" to celebrate Abraham Lincoln's birthday. The hymn is first performed by 500 children at Stanton School in Jacksonville, Florida.

1902 — James resigns from Stanton School. James and John move to New York City and write songs for Broadway.

1905 — James supports the Niagara Movement, a group that works for fairness and equal rights for Black people.

1906 - 1910 — James becomes a U.S. diplomat, traveling to countries including Venezuela and Nicaragua to represent the United States.

1910 — James marries Grace Nail.

1912 — James writes The Autobiography of an Ex-Colored Man, a powerful novel about race and identity.

1913 — John marries Nora Ethel Floyd. They have two children.

1914 — John is appointed the director of New York's Music School Settlement for Colored People.

1917 — James and John lead the Silent Protest Parade in response to the East St. Louis massacre.

1919 — "Lift Every Voice and Sing" is adopted as the official song of the NAACP (National Association for the Advancement of Colored People).

1920 — James becomes the first Black leader of the NAACP.

1925 - 1926 — James and John write, The Book of American Negro Spirtuals, in two volumes.

1935 — John performs in George Gershwin's Porgy and Bess. He sings the role of Frazier in the original production.

1938 — James Weldon Johnson passes away at the age of sixty-seven in a car accident in Wiscasset, Maine.

1954 — John Rosamond Johnson passes away at the age of eighty-one.

ACKNOWLEDGEMENTS

Telling this story of James and John Johnson has been an incredible journey, and I could not have done it alone.

Thank you to CJ Love — you filled these pages with artistic detail that brought James and John to life with historical accuracy and made the book accessible and engaging for all readers. Your illustrations honor the brothers' legacy beautifully.

To Christy Witte — thank you for your steady guidance, reassurance, and belief in the power of this story from the very beginning.

To the amazing team at Two Penny Publishing — thank you for walking with me every step of the way and helping this dream become a gift for the Stanton community.

A special thanks to Una Whitley — for your thoughtful contributions and, most of all, for your friendship. You help shape the way I see the world, and you remain a constant example of what it truly means to love and stand beside students.

To BreeAnna Haynes — thank you for connecting this story to our beloved students and families in such meaningful ways. Your deep connection with students has always been my example of what it means to teach with heart.

To Joanne Williams, Linda Kuzmack, JaRonda Dockett, and Dr. Raymond Wise — your thoughtful edits and encouragement helped this book become its best self. Thank you.

To Dr. Ruth T. Reyes — you believed in a book before I did.

To Stanton Elementary School — you have given me a home where I am honored to teach, grow, and love students, and where I am continually reminded of the power of community, resilience, and hope.

And to Khaliq, my student editor — your voice reminds me who this book is really for. Thank you for sharing your brilliance.

Finally, I give thanks to God, who is the source of every good gift. To Him be the glory.

ABOUT THE AUTHOR

Chad Harris is a music teacher and author who has spent twenty years helping students discover the joy of learning through music. He has taught in Florida, Alabama, and South Korea, and now he shares his love of music with the amazing students at Stanton Elementary School in Southeast Washington, DC. Mr. Harris encourages his students to use their talents to bring joy, healing, and hope to the world. This book was written with his students in mind, especially those whose voices deserve to be lifted and celebrated.